Thank you to the generous team who gave their time and talents to make this book possible:

Author
Worku L. Mulat

Illustrator
Daniel Getahun

Editor
Beth Bacon

Creative Directors
Caroline Kurtz, Jane Kurtz, and Kenny Rasmussen

Translators
Yoseph Ayalew
Woubeshet Ayenew

Designer
Beth Crow and Kenny Rasmussen

Ready Set Go Books, an Open Hearts Big Dreams Project

Special thanks to Ethiopia Reads donors and staff for believing in this project and helping get it started-- and for arranging printing, distribution, and training in Ethiopia.

Copyright © 2020 Ready Set Go Books

ISBN: 979-8718586787
Library of Congress Control Number: 2021904698

All rights reserved. No part of this book may be reproduced, scanned or distributed in any printed or electronic form without permission.
Printed in Seattle, WA, U.S.A.

Publication Date: 03/10/21

The Cheetahs of Long Distance Running in Ethiopia

የኢትዮጵያ ታላቅ ሯጮች
- አቦ ሼማኔዎቹ

English and Amharic

Cheetahs are among the fastest animals in the world. They can run up to 120 kilometers per hour, which is about 80 miles per hour. Many cheetahs live in Ethiopia. And guess what? Some of the fastest humans in the world live in Ethiopia, too. That is why Ethiopian runners call themselves "cheetahs." Let's meet some cheetahs from Ethiopia.

አቦ ሻማኔ ከአለም ፈጣን እንሰሳት መሃል አንዱ ነው። በሰዓት እስከ 120 ኪ.ሜ ወይም 80 ማይል መሮጥ ይችላል። በርካታ አቦ ሻማኔዎች በኢትዮጵያ ውስጥ ይኖራሉ። እንዲሁም ከዓለም በሩጫ ፈጣን ከሆኑት ሰዎች መሃል አንዳንዶቹ በኢትዮጵያ ውስጥ ይኖራሉ። ለዚህ ነው ኢትዮጵውያን ራጮች ራሳቸውን አቦ ሻማኔ ብለው የሚጠሩት። እስቲ አንዳንድ የኢትዮጵያ አቦሻማኔዎችን እንተዋወቅ።

Abebe Bikila set the bar high when he became the cheetah of his generation. In 1960, he was celebrated as the first black African Olympic gold medalist. He won his first Olympic marathon running barefoot through the streets of Rome and his second, four years later in Tokyo.

አበበ በቂላ የሮጫቸነትን ክብር ከፍተኛ ደረጃ ያደረሰ የትውልዱ የመጀመሪያው አቦሻማኔ ነበር። በ1960 አበበ በቂላ በኦለምፒክ መድረክ የመጀመሪያውን ጥቁር አፍሪካዊ የወርቅ ሜዳሊያ ተሸላሚ ሆነ። የጀመሪያውን የኦሎምፒክ ማራቶን ውድድር በሮም ከተማ በባዶ እግሩ ተወዳድሮ አሸነፈ፤ ከአራት አመት በኋላ በቶክዮ ለሁለተኛ ጊዜ ማራቶን ደጋሞ በማሸነፍ የኦሎምፒክ ታሪክ ውስጥ ስሙን አስቀርጿል።

Mamo Wolde was another cheetah in Abebe Bikila's generation. When Abebe dropped out of the marathon in the 1968 Olympics—due to a stress fracture—Mamo went on to win the gold medal. That way, Ethiopians won the Olympics marathon three times in a row.

ማሞ ወልዴ ሌላኛው በእነአበበ በቂላ ትውልድ የነበረ አቦ ሺማኔ ነው። አበበ በቂላ እግሩን ተሰብሮ ከውድድሩ ውጭ ሲሆን ማሞ ወልዴ እሱን ተክቶ በ1968 በሜክሲኮ በተደረገው አለምፒክ በማራቶን የወርቅ ሜዳሊያ ተሸላሚ ሆኗል። በአበበና በማሞ አቦ ሺማኔነት፣ የኦሊምፒክ ማራቶንን በተከታታይ ሶስቴ ያሸነፈች አገር ኢትዮጵያ ብቻ ናት።

Miruts Yifter was another great athlete. His nickname was the Shifter—can you guess why? Miruts was known to defeat opponents by shifting into a faster speed near the finish line. Miruts Yifter won two gold medals at the 1980 Summer Olympics.

ምሩፅ ይፍጠር ሌላኛው ታላቅ ሯጭ ነበር፤ ቅጽል ስሙም ማርሽ ቀያሪው ነበር። ለምን እንደሆነ ታውቃላችሁ? ምሩጽ ተቀናቃኞቹን በመጨረሻው ዙር ላይ በድንገት ፍጥነት በመጨመር ስለሚያሸንፋቸው ነበር። ምሩጽ ይፍጠር በ1980 በተደረገው አሎምፒክ ላይ 2 የወርቅ ሜዳሊያ ተሸላሚ ሆኗል።

Belayneh Densamo is a long distance runner who won three major marathons between 1986 and 1996. In the Rotterdam marathon in 1988, he broke the world record. Belayneh held that world record for a long time—10 years.

በላይነህ ዲንሳሞ ሌላው አቦ ሸማኔ ሲሆን ከ1986 እስከ 1996 ሶስት ታላላቅ የማራቶን ውድድሮችን አሸንፏል። በሮተርዳም በ1988 ላይ በተደረገው የማራቶን ውድድር የአለም ክብረ ወሰንን ሰብሯል፤ ይህም ክብረ ወሰን ለ10 ዓመታት ሳይሰበር ቆይቷል።

Haile Gebrselassie is recognized by many as the greatest athlete of all time because he broke 27 world records. As a child, he ran barefoot to school and back, just like his role model Abebe Bikila, and later often raced as if his left arm was holding school books. He won his first international races in youth competitions. Later, he won two Olympic gold medals and four world championship titles.

ሃይሌ ገብረስላሴ በብዙዎች ዘንድ የዓለም ታላቅ አትሌትነቱ የሚታወቅ 27 የዓለም የሩጫ ከብረወሰኖችን የሰበረ አቦ ሻማኔ ነው። ሃይሌ ገብረስላሴ ልክ እንደዓርአያው አበበ በቂላ ከቤት ወደ ትምህርት ቤትና መልስ በባዶ እግሩ ይሮጥ ነበር። ሃይሌ ብዙውን ጊዜ ሲሮጥ በግራ እጁ የትምህርት ቤት መጽሐፉን እንደያዘ ሰው ይመስላል። የመጀመሪያውን ዓለም አቀፍ ውድድር ያሸነፈው በወጣቶች ዘርፍ በተደረገው ውድድር ሲሆን በማስከተልም ሁለት ጊዜ የኦሎምፒክ ወርቅ ሜዳሊያ እና አራት ጊዜ የዓለም ሻምፒዮና ሜዳሊያ ተሸላሚ ነበር።

Kenenisa Bekele became the cheetah of the next generation. He broke the world record for the 2000-meter indoor competition in 2007. Kenenisa won several gold medals and set many world records. The name Kenenisa Bekele became known throughout the world.

ቀነኒሳ በቀለ የቀጣዩ ትውልድ አቦ ሻማኔ ነበር። ቀነኒሳ በ2000 ሜትር ውድድር የዓለም ክብረ ወሰንን በ2007 ሰብሯል። በብዙ ውድድሮች የወርቅ ሜዳሊያ ያገኘ ሲሆን በተጨማሪም ብዙ ክብረወሰኖችን ሰብሯል። በዚህም ምክንያት የቀነኒሳ በቀለ ስም በመላው ዓለም ላይ ታዋቂነትን አግኝቷል።

The beginning of the 1990's saw the rise of a female running star in Africa. Derartu Tulu, who grew up tending her family's cattle in Bekoji, Ethiopia became a strong female cheetah of her generation. She was the first black African woman to win an Olympic gold medal--in the 10,000-meter event in 1992. After the birth of a daughter, she came back to run again, ending up with a total of 6 world and Olympic gold medals.

በ1990ዎቹ መጀመሪያ ላይ ኮኮብ አፍሪካዊ ሴት ሯጮች መታየት ጀመሩ። በበቆጂ ከተማ የቤተሰቦቿን ከብቶች ስትጠብቅ ያደገችው ደራርቱ ቱሉ በዘመኗ ጠንካራ የሴት አበ ሻማኔ ነበረች። ደራርቱ በ1992 በኦሎምፒክ መድረክ ላይ በ10000 ሜትር ወርቅ ሜዳሊያ ስትረከብ የመጀመሪያዋ ጥቁር አፍሪካዊ የስፖርቱ ተሸላሚ ሆነች። ልጅ ከወለደች በኋላም ወደ ሩጫው አለም ተመልሳ 6 ጊዜ የአለም ሻምፒዮና እና የኦሎምፒክ ወርቅ ሜዳሊያ አሸንፋለች።

Meseret Defar is the female cheetah who followed in the footsteps of Derartu Tulu. She broke a world record in 2006. A year later, she broke her own world record! Meseret was the first female to run a two-mile race in less than 10 minutes.

She became a star of her generation and a role model for girls in Africa.

መሰረት ደፋር የደራርቱ ቱሉን ዱካ የተከትላለች ሴላዋ ሴት አቦ ሻማኔ ነበረች። በ2006 የዓለምን 5000 ሜትር ውድድር ክብር ወሰነን የሰበረች ሲሆን ከአንድ አመት በኋላ ደግማ የራሷን ክብረወሰን አሻሽላለች። መሰረት የሁለት ማይሎች ውድድርን ከ10 ደቂቃ በታች ስትጨርስ የመጀመሪያዋ ሴት ነች። መሰረት የዘመኗ ኮከብ ከመሆኗም በላይ ለአፈሪካ ወጣት ሴቶች መልካም አርአያ ሆናለች።

Inspired by her cousin Derartu Tulu, Tirunesh Debaba worked hard to become a top runner. She began competing as a 14-year-old, earning the nickname "The Baby Faced Destroyer" and became the youngest World Champion runner at 18 years old. In the 2008 Olympics, she became the first female cheetah to win gold in both the 5,000-meter and 10,000-meter races.

ጥሩነሽ ዲባባ በአክስቲ በደራርቱ ቱሉ ምሳሌነት ታላቅ ሯጭ ለመሆን በቅታለች። ጥሩነሽ ውድድር የጀመረችው በ14 ዓመቷ ሲሆን "ድል አድራጊዋ ወጣት" የሚል ቅጽል ስም የተሰጣት ሯጭ በአለም ሻምፒዮና ውድድር በ18 ዓመቷ ስትሳተፍ የሁሉም የእድሜ ታናሽ አትሌት ነበረች። በ2008 አሎምፒክ በ5000 ሜትር እና በ10000 ሜትር ውድድር የአሎምፒክ ወርቅ ሜዳሊያ ተሸላሚ የመጀመሪያዋ ሴት አቦሸማኔ ሆናለች።

Genzebe Dibaba made track history, holding the most world records by one person. She is the younger sister of Turnesh and Ejeagayehu Dibaba and a niece of Deratu Tulu. Her athleticism helped cement her family as a dominant force in women's running--a whole family of cheetahs!

ገንዘቤ ዲባባ በሩጫ ታሪክ ከሌላ ሰው በላይ ክብረወሰኖችን በመያዝ ትታወቃለች። ገንዘቤ የጥሩነሽ እና የእጅጋየሁ ዲባባ ታናሽ እህት ስትሆን የደራርቱ ቱሉ የእህት ልጅ ነችም። የእሷ ውጤታማነት በሴቶች የሩጫ ውድድር ላይ የቤተቦቿን አንጋፋነት አረጋግጧል - የአቦ ሼማኔ ቤተሰብ!

Ethiopia's elite runners are sleek, swift, and graceful. And like the mighty cheetah, their strength and speed will continue to be admired around the world as future generations come and go.

የኢትዮጵያ አንጋፋ ሯጮች ፍጥነት እና ደስ የሚያሰኝ ሞገስ የተጎናጸፉ ናቸው። ልክ እንደ ኃያሉ አቦሽማኔ ፍጥነታቸው እና ጥንካሬያቸው በወደፊቱም ትውልድ በአለም ላይ እየተደነቀ ይቀጥላል።

About The Story

In 1960, Abebe Bikala made history as the first black African Olympic gold medalist—and he did it by running barefoot because his new shoes didn't fit well. In an interesting 2020 twist, another Ethiopian runner set a course record at the Dubai marathon, even though he had never run a marathon before and had to borrow shoes from another runner (after his were lost on the flight).

Haile Gebrselassie made history of a different kind by breaking those twenty-seven world records and becoming a legendary runner. You can see more of his story here: https://www.olympicchannel.com/en/video/detail/where-are-they-now-haile-gebrselassie-s-legend-lives-on/

When Fatuma Roba was growing up, Abebe Bikila was her only role model. She became the first woman from an African nation to ever win the Olympic women's marathon (in Atlanta Summer Olympics). The documentary "Town of Runners" shows how she, Kenenisa Bekele, Tirunesh Dibaba, and Derartu Tulu, all Ethiopian Olympic gold medal-winning runners, come from one town—Bekoji. Their stories are included here: https://www.theguardian.com/sport/2012/apr/06/ethiopian-home-worlds-greatest-runners along with information about the coach who trained them and went on to work with the latest generation of champions – Tirunesh's sister Genzebe and Kenenisa's younger brother Tariku who won the 3000m gold at the World Indoor Championships.

Another article about the Dibaba family can be read here: https://www.vogue.com/article/dibaba-family-ethiopian-distance-runners-olympics-2016-rio-de-janeiro

Every year, new Ethiopian runners set records. For example, in the 2016 Olympics, Almaz Ayana smashed the women's world record in the 10,000 meter race--just the second time she had attempted that race on a track--and became a new role model for many young Ethiopian runners. Who will be next?

About the Author

Dr. Mulat was born and grew up in a remote village called Kersole, South Wollo, Ethiopia to parents who never had the opportunity to learn how to read or to write. Drought happened often and frost frequently killed crops. Dr. Mulat vividly remembers the economic woes of his rural village. His parents were determined their children would break the cycle of poverty through unlocking the power of education. But it wasn't simple or easy. The family still needed his support, so attending elementary school needed to be balanced with farming. With his mother's strong encouragement, he excelled at school (and farming), becoming a role model to his brothers and sisters, earning advanced degrees in Biology, Environmental Sanitation and Applied Ecology. His parents, who never set foot in school, have seen all their children graduated with advanced degrees in Physics, Computer Science, Chemistry and Math.

Dr. Mulat and his family proved poverty was neither in the genes nor in the stars; rather, by taking advantage of every learning opportunity, he made poverty history for his household. His diverse life experiences have taken him to Europe, Texas, and Washington State. Dr Mulat has a strong passion to pay back to his village and others around Ethiopia through promoting literacy, innovation and education. Becoming a children's book author for kids who too rarely get to see themselves in books and sharing the rich history and culture of his birth are just some of the ways he is working to pay it forward.

About the Illustrator

Daniel Getahun lives in Toronto, Canada. He received a diploma in graphic art from Addis Ababa School of Fine Arts and Design in 1980. He now focuses on oil painting and digital painting, which can be seen on his Facebook page. He can also be contacted by email: danielgetahun1@hotmail.com

About The Editor

Beth Abate Bacon is an author of books for young people. She earned an MFA in writing for children from Vermont College of Fine Arts. She also has a degree in communications from NYU and a degree in literature from Harvard. She previously worked with Apple on communications and marketing, as well as a teacher at the elementary and high school levels. Beth loves to travel and share stories about our world's varied cultures, traditions, and perspectives.

About Ethiopia Reads

Ethiopia Reads was started by volunteers in places like Grand Forks, North Dakota; Denver, Colorado; San Francisco, California; and Washington D.C. who wanted to give the gift of reading to more kids in Ethiopia.

One of the founders, Jane Kurtz, learned to read in Ethiopia where she spent most of her childhood and where the circle of life has come around to bring her Ethiopian-American grandchildren. As a children's book author, Jane is the driving force behind Open Hearts Big Dreams Ready Set Go Books - working to create the books that inspire those just learning to read.

About Open Hearts Big Dreams

Open Hearts Big Dreams began as a volunteer organization, led by Ellenore Angelidis in Seattle, Washington, to provide sustainable funding and strategic support to Ethiopia Reads, collaborating with Jane Kurtz. OHBD has now grown to be its own nonprofit organization supporting literacy, innovation, and leadership for young people in Ethiopia.

Ellenore Angelidis comes from a family of teachers who believe education is a human right, and opportunity should not depend on your birthplace. And as the adoptive mother of a little girl who was born in Ethiopia and learned to read in the U.S., as well as an aspiring author, she finds the chance to positively impact literacy hugely compelling!

About Ready Set Go Books

Reading has the power to change lives, but many children and adults in Ethiopia cannot read. One reason is that Ethiopia doesn't have enough books in local languages to give people a chance to practice reading. Ready Set Go books wants to close that gap and open a world of ideas and possibilities for kids and their communities.

When you buy a Ready Set Go book, you provide critical funding to create and distribute more books.

Learn more at: http://openheartsbigdreams.org/book-project/

Ready Set Go 10 Books

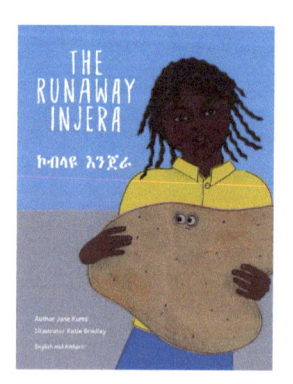

In 2018, Ready Set Go Books decided to experiment by trying a few new books in larger sizes.

Sometimes it was the art that needed a little more room to really shine. Sometimes the story or nonfiction text was a bit more complicated than the short and simple text used in most of our current early reader books.

We called these our "Ready Set Go 10" books as a way to show these ones are bigger and also sometimes have more words on the page. The response has been great so now our Ready Set Go 10 books are a significant number of our titles. We are happy to hear feedback on these new books and on all our books.

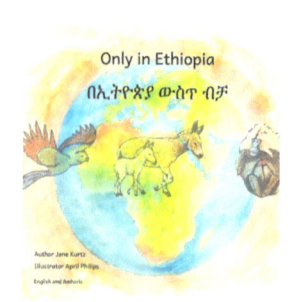

About the Language

Amharic is a Semetic language -- in fact, the world's second-most widely spoken Semetic language, after Arabic. Starting in the 12th century, it became the Ethiopian language that was used in official transactions and schools and became widely spoken all over Ethiopia. It's written with its own characters, over 260 of them. Eritrea and Ethiopia share this alphabet, and they are the only countries in Africa to develop a writing system centuries ago that is still in use today!

About the Translation

Yoseph Ayalew is a primary school teacher by training with a special interest in supporting the development of orphans and vulnerable children (OVC). In 2000 he founded a private school (MYFV Academy) offering kindergarten to grade 8 classes. MYFV provided a total of 54 FREE learning opportunities for orphans and vulnerable children; 15 of them funded by MYFV and 39 funded by an American NGO. In 2006, in collaboration with Volunteer Services Overseas (VSO), a UK NGO, Yoseph published his first children's book on HIV/AIDS. All books were distributed FREE to schools in Addis Ababa and throughout Ethiopia. In 2012, he published 2 books: "50 Answers to Children's Questions About HIV/AIDS" in collaboration with Ethiopia Reads, USA; and "The Loss of Innocence" in collaboration with People to People (P2P) Canada. Since 2011, Yoseph has been organizing a children's festival at the Addis Ababa Exhibition Center to celebrate the International Day of African Child.

Dr. Woubeshet Ayenew's role at Ready Set Go Books combines his passions for parenting and language. He is a cardiologist by training but parenting is his most demanding and wonderfully rewarding job. Once his children started to read and write in Amharic, he went out searching for child-friendly bilingual books. He eventually linked up with the creative team from Ready Set Go Books.

Though a resident of the US for over 30 years, he maintains a healthy grasp of his native language and culture; his shelves are filled with Amharic novels and other writings that he picks up during his regular medical mission trips to Ethiopia, and he assumes many roles in his Ethiopian community in Minnesota. He views every story in the Ready Set Go Books collection from the side of his Ethiopian-American children as well as from the perspective of the young readers of his native land. He knows the job is done when there is something wondrous for everyone in every story.

Over 100 unique Ready Set Go books available!

To view all available titles, search "Ready Set Go Ethiopia" or scan QR code

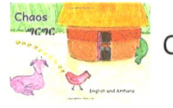

- Chaos
- Talk Talk Turtle 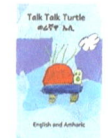
- The Glory of Gondar 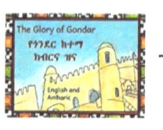
- We Can Stop the Lion 
- Not Ready! 
- Fifty Lemons 
- Count For Me 
- Too Brave 
- Tell Me What You Hear 

Open Heart Big Dreams is pleased to offer discounts for bulk orders, educators and organizations.

Contact ellenore@openheartsbigdreams.org for more information.

Ready Set Go Books

OPEN HEARTS BIG DREAMS

CPSIA information can be obtained
at www.ICGtesting.com
Printed in the USA
LVHW071330011121
702129LV00014B/209